To God or from Irene

You are never too young or old to do something new. All my life I have loved to write stories and poems. I have never before had a book published. Now that I am old (great-grandma old), my dreams have come true. So never give up hoping and dreaming, because it is never too late.

Irene Bartlett

THE OLD TESTAMENT
Bible Poems for Children

The Old Testament

Bible Poems for Children

Irene Bartlett

ATHENA PRESS
LONDON

ISBN 10-digit: 1 84748 204 X
ISBN 13-digit: 978 1 84748 204 4

First Published 2007 by
ATHENA PRESS
Queen's House, 2 Holly Road
Twickenham TW1 4EG
United Kingdom

Printed for Athena Press

Note from the Author

This book of stories from the Bible, told in verse, is suitable
for children to hear and understand at a very young age.
Hopefully, they will want to return to it over and over again
as they grow older, and then in turn read it to their own
children.

These poems are intended to be read aloud to children by
their parents, grandparents and teachers. When children are
old enough to read, they should be encouraged to read them
aloud themselves. They will become familiar with verse and
grow to love it, as I did, and as my children did when they
were young.

My thanks go to:

Angela Flexen, for spending many hours of her time doing the black and white drawings that illustrate each story, and for her encouragement and guidance.

To all my friends for their encouragement.

To my family, who believed that I could achieve my dreams.

To the staff and children from Victoria Road Infant School in Cirencester, who inspired me and who rejoiced in my success.

Mainly, my thanks go to God and the Holy Spirit, for inspiring me to write these poems, and for giving me the talent to do so.

I dedicate this work to my daughter, Jane (the miracle that God worked for me); to my son, Christopher; and to the memory of my late husband, Chris.

Contents

In the Beginning

God looked down from heaven
And there was nothing there at all.
Then he chose a place out in space
And he placed there a big black ball.

'This land will be Earth,' God said with delight,
'And I will make it a beautiful place.
So first I'll make light, shining bright,
And then I'll make a human race.'

And so he made the sun to shine,
Warming the earth and giving it light.
Then he made the moon to glow,
To lighten up the night.

He made the soft falling rains
Which fell upon the hard dry plains;
These formed rivers and gentle streams,
Twinkling and sparkling in the sun's beams.

God said, 'I need colour in this land.'
And so from the earth below,
Wonderful grass and flowers grew;
Their colours all aglow.

Oranges, yellows, reds and some blue;
Shades of green and pink and purple too.
Then up sprang trees growing so high,
And God put the blue into the sky.

When all this was ready God spoke again and said,
'We must have things to live here.
Lions, horses and tigers striped black and red
Elephants and crocodiles, rabbits and deer.'
And so all the animals started to appear.

Then God said, 'Come forth, all you flying things,
Birds and insects too.'
There were doves and parrots with shiny wings,
Swallows and swifts, spiders, and caterpillars too.

God saw the seas and rivers and he had a wish;
He spoke the words, waved his hand, and then there
    were fish.
Some small tiddlers, some cod and herring too;
There were salmon and sharks, and dolphins, and a
    whale or two.

Now came God's most important plan;
Now was the time for him to make man.
God called his name and from the dust he came,
And God spoke to Adam, for that was his name.

'I will give you a woman to share your life.'
And so he made Eve to be Adam's wife.
'And you will live in obedience and grace,
And be happy evermore in this wonderful place.'

The Broken Promise – Adam and Eve

God had given Adam and Eve
A wonderful place to live.
It was a special gift for them,
The best that God could give.

'I want you to be happy here,
In this most beautiful place;
For here there is no room for sin,
You will live in a state of grace.'

Adam smiled at Eve,
Whatever could he say?
'We will thank God together
On this bright and lovely day.'

So they spoke to God
And he told them what to do,
'Look after all the animals,
And I'll look after you.

'I will give you fruit to eat
And nuts from the walnut tree;
Just tend my garden,
And I'll love you, as you love me.

'There is just one thing I must ask;
It isn't hard to do.
There is just one tree in the garden
Which doesn't belong to you.

'That fruit tree in the middle
With fruit that looks good to eat;
I do not wish you to taste it,
It is bitter, it is not sweet.

'If you disobey me then you will see
Not only the things that are beautiful and good,
But bad things, evil things
And temptations here in the wood.'

So Adam and Eve avoided the tree
And lived in perfect harmony.
Until one day – *alas!* –
A serpent slithered through the grass.

He spied Eve sitting on her own
And he smiled as he spoke to her alone,
'Tell me,' he said, with a nasty leer,
'Which fruit do you eat when you are here?'

'Why all the fruit is ours to have our fill,
Except the one that would make us ill.
God says we are not to eat it, for it is bad,
And that would make God very sad.'

'Oh nonsense,' said that nasty snake,
Giving his head a very good shake,
'That fruit will bring you lots of wealth.
But God just wants it for himself.'

So Eve picked an apple from the tree;
It looked very good as she could see.
She took it back for Adam so that he could see it,
And together they sat on the grass and ate it.

When they next saw God they were very afraid;
They knew now what a mistake they had made.
They wanted to run away and hide,
But God appeared by their side.

'I know,' said God, 'just what you have done.
You must leave the garden now, and from now on
Life will not be so easy for you.
You will have to work hard your whole life through.

And when your lives come to an end –
And some day I'm afraid they must –
Then you will return, whence you came,
To the ground, to become dust.'

So Adam and Eve walked away
Knowing that they had to learn to obey.
Maybe God one day would forgive
And would help them once again to live.

Building a Boat – Noah

God was feeling very sad;
The people down on earth were very bad.
They were neglecting the whole place;
It was becoming a terrible disgrace.

Fields were left, no seeds were sown,
No fruit and berries were being grown.
People were fighting, sister and brother,
All of them seemed to be hating each other.

God was unhappy at what he had seen;
He needed the world to be washed clean.
One thing was certainly plain –
He needed to start all over again.

Then he saw Noah, who was not like the rest.
He was good and kind, he was the best.
'Noah and his family I will save.
It will be hard for him, but he is brave.'

God told Noah to build a big boat;
Big and strong so that it would float.
'You will be sailing a very long way
So make preparations for that day.

'You will take with you your wife,
For you will be starting a whole new life.
Your three sons and their wives will go too;
Your daughters with their husbands will sail with
    you.

'Of every animal, take two:
Lions and tigers and kangaroo,
Pigs and horses, cows and cats,
Dogs and elephants, squirrels and bats.'

Now all the people thought it was sad;
They said that Noah was going mad.
To build a boat was stupid you see,
When they lived miles and miles from the sea.

But Noah did what God had said,
Praying every night when he went to bed
That God would guide him, and show the way,
And God did that the very next day.

For the boat was now ready, and they all climbed
    aboard,
All the birds and the animals in happy accord.
God closed the door, and they were warm and snug,
Noah and his family wrapped in a rug.

Then God sent the rain every day and night;
Not a dry patch of land was there in sight.
It rained for forty nights and days;
There was no sign of the sun's rays.

It rained so hard, that it rocked their boat,
And they found themselves afloat.
And as the seas filled, the boat lifted way up high;
It seemed to be reaching right up to the sky.

Then the rain stopped and the sun came out;
Noah and his family began to shout.
They rushed up on deck to see water all around;
It was quiet, and still, there was not a sound.

They could see no land, just sea below and sky
   above,
So Noah sent out a small bird called a dove.
When the dove did not return Noah knew
It had found a place to build a nest anew.

Then the earth began to dry and the seas slowly fell,
And God told Noah that all was well.
They were on the top of a mountain high,
With land all around them that was dry.

Everywhere looked fresh and new,
The colours shone with every hue,
A rainbow glowed in the sky,
As the sun shone way up high.

Noah and his family thanked God for their lives;
He had helped them all to survive.
And now they could start life all anew,
Knowing that is what God wanted them to do.

God looked and he smiled, for he was happy too;
He had washed the world to make it new.

The Tall Tower of Babel

God looked down from heaven
At a land called Shinar
And he watched building going on.
Bricks and cement everywhere, near and far.

People were building a tower
With walls very high,
'I wonder what they are up to,'
He thought with a sigh.

He listened to them talking, as they were working,
And they seemed to be making quite a to do.
They were all laughing and singing happily,
And understood each other easily.

But one man looked quite confused
And looking up at the sky,
He asked the man next to him,
'Why are we building it so high?'

'I think that is the idea.
I have heard the word
That when it is finished it will be
The tallest tower in the world.

'And when the people pass this way,
They will look up in surprise.
They will be so amazed
They won't believe their eyes.

'They will say that these men are clever,
And they will remark and say with a sigh,
"God himself could not have built,
Such a wonder, way up high." '

Well God heard all this;
He thought about what they had said
And he smiled to himself.
Then an idea came into his head.

'I will give them different languages
And then we shall see
Just how clever they really are,
And if they are brighter than me.'

So next time God listened
To what they had to say.
He sat back and watched
As his plan went this way.

First of all the man on top of the tower
Called to his friend,
'Pass me some cement, and another trowel.'
And his friend replied, 'Por qué?' And he said it with
    a scowl.

'What are you talking about?'
Said the man from up on high.
'I do not understand you.'
And he gave a great big sigh.

'Excuse me,' said another man
To a workman passing down below,
'Please lend me your hammer,
We have a lot higher to go.'

The man answered with some sort of jumble,
The words all of a bungle.
It sounded as though he was saying,
'You are like a donkey braying.'

Everyone was making such a din,
Talking in strange ways, not understanding any-
thing,
They just stood still wondering.

Some were talking in Greek,
And some in Italian,
Some in French or English,
But it all sounded like gibberish.

And so it was, all over the place,
The work slowed down to a very slow pace.
No one could understand what the others were say-
ing
And the tall tower started swaying.

The men put down their buckets and their bricks,
They were fed up with these tricks.
If they could not understand each other
They couldn't go on, so why should they bother?

And when other people passed by,
They didn't admire a tower as high as the sky.
Instead they pointed to all the rubble,
And they laughed and said, 'Hay hubble wubble'.

And if you want to know
What they had said,
It was that we should leave God
To work his wonders instead.

Abraham

Abraham was a very rich man
Who lived in a wonderful place called Haran.
He owned lots of camels, and lots of sheep,
And he had a wonderful house in which to sleep.

With Sarah, his wife, by his side,
He could look all around him with lots of pride.
There was only one thing he would have wished for:
Just one son or a daughter, or maybe more.

But alas, this was not to be!
For Abraham and Sarah were old you see.
But they were happy and contented with their life,
And Abraham thanked God for a wonderful wife.

Although he could not see him, Abraham knew God
    was there,
And each night he spoke to God in a prayer.
He thanked him for blessings given to him,
And sometimes he even sang him a hymn.

Now, one cold, dark and starry night,
God spoke to Abraham, much to his delight.
But when he heard what God had to say,
His face looked sad, and he said with dismay,

'I'm not really sure that I heard you right,
Maybe I'm going deaf this very night.
I thought you had asked me to move far away,
And I really do not know what to say.'

But God spoke again and Abraham knew
Just what God wanted him to do.
'Dear God,' he asked, 'where is it and how far?'
God said, 'Just pack your things, I will tell you
    where.'

And when all was made ready, it was bright and
    sunny,
God said they were off to a land of milk and honey.
'A land called Canaan is where I want you to be,
And I have plans for you and Sarah, just wait and
    see.'

And that night when Abraham spoke to God in
    prayer,
There was a stillness and quiet in the air.
'Look up, Abraham, at the stars above.
One day you will have as many children to love.'

Abraham laughed, and replied with glee,
'God, you know you are teasing me.
Look at me God, I am old and grey;
How can I have children anyway?'

'Look down at the sand,' God replied.
Abraham did as God told him and sighed,
'What is there to see, God? Just grains of sand.'
'That's how many children of yours will live in this
    land.

'One day Abraham you will have a son,
And through him wonderful things will be done.'
Well Abraham told Sarah what God had said,
And he giggled and laughed as he got into bed.

Abraham and Sarah settled in Canaan
And there was peace and tranquillity all around
them.
And one year later, Sarah gave birth to a son,
Much to the surprise of everyone.

He brought much joy to them ever after,
And they called him Isaac, which is Hebrew for
laughter.
And God in heaven smiled on them that day,
For he had planned it all to happen this way.

Two Brothers – Jacob and Esau

Isaac had two sons, Jacob and Esau, who were not
    alike at all.
Esau was short, fat and hairy; Jacob big and tall.
Esau worked very hard, while Jacob was pampered
    and idle.
Esau did all the work, while Jacob did very little.

Isaac loved his two sons, but he loved Esau more.
While Rebecca, Isaac's wife, her son Jacob she did adore.
Jacob idled all his time sitting with his mother;
He lied and he cheated and he hated his brother.

Isaac had grown very old, and the poor man was blind.
Esau loved his father, for he was very kind.
One day Isaac asked Esau to go and kill a goat,
And cook it for him in a stewing pot.

Isaac said, 'When you have done that, come and eat
    with me,
I know that I will die soon, and I will let you see
All the things I will leave you after I have gone,
Because I love you, you are my beloved son.'

Now Rebecca heard what was said and she was very
    angry.
She sent for Jacob to come to her and she sat at his
    knee.
'You must pretend to be Esau so that you will know
    just where
Isaac has put his precious things when he is no
    longer there.'

So Jacob did as his mother said, and wore a hairy
coat,
While Rebecca made a tasty stew with a freshly-
killed goat.
And before Esau could return Jacob stood before his
father
And said, 'Just as you told me, I have brought your
food, dear father.'

Now Isaac was blind, and could not see his son,
But there was something about his voice that
seemed wrong.
'Let me feel your arms, son,' Isaac said, and he felt
the hairy coat.
It must be Esau, Isaac thought, and they sat and ate
the goat.

Then Isaac made a promise, thinking it was to Esau
he was making it,
'When I am gone, you will inherit all my land, and
everything in it.
You will be in charge of all the family, so look after
your mother;
See that she is cared for, and do what you can for
your brother.'

Just then the door opened and Esau came rushing to
Isaac's side.
'I am back Father, I've caught a lovely goat,' he said
with pride.
Isaac cried with dismay when he realised he had
been cheated,
And far into the night, their argument was heated.

Once a promise had been made, it could not be
  unmade,
And as Esau listened, he knew that Isaac must be
  obeyed.
'I will kill my brother one day,' he vowed,
But God had other plans, so that could not be
  allowed.

Jacob was afraid of Esau, and didn't really want to
  stay,
So in the night he fled, he would run far away.
He knew that he had cheated his brother,
So he left his home, his father and his mother.

Jacob

Jacob had to run, run, run;
He was very tired, and it wasn't much fun.
He had cheated brother Esau, and he was afraid;
He realised what a mistake he had made.

God watched him from up on high;
He knew what Jacob had done, and he gave a sigh.
Jacob lay down exhausted, in a heap,
He closed his eyes and fell asleep.

God sent Jacob a special dream;
The tallest ladder he had ever seen.
With angels climbing up and down,
Each angel clothed in a white gown.

And when Jacob looked up into the sky,
At the top of the ladder was God on high.
God spoke to Jacob, 'You want to know who I am?
I am the God of your father Isaac and your grand-
    father Abraham.

'I made them a promise and it is yours too;
This is what I intend for you.
This land I will give you, if you learn to obey,
Now wake up and I will go with you on your way.'

When Jacob awoke he seemed to be all alone.
But Jacob knew God would never be gone.
He left a stone to mark the holy place
Where God had forgiven him for his disgrace.

He ran on to the house of his uncle, Laban.
And God kept watch as Jacob ran.
Soon Jacob would have a lesson to learn;
Something would happen to cause him concern.

Uncle Laban took Jacob in and introduced his
    daughters with a grin,
For here was the son-in-law made for him.
Leah was the eldest of the girls,
With hair like silk and beautiful curls.

But it was Rachel, the youngest, that caught Jacob's
    eye;
Her angelic smile made him sigh.
He asked Uncle Laban if they could be married,
Laban pondered the question, and tarried.

Then he spoke to Jacob and this is what he said,
'Before you and Rachel can be wed
You must work seven years on my land.
Then I'll be happy to give you her hand.'

And so Jacob toiled from morning until night;
Knowing that the end would soon be in sight.
Then came the day when he stood beside his bride
And he smiled as he held her hand with pride.

But when he lifted the veil from her face,
He saw it was Leah, in Rachel's place.
He was angry and he shouted at Laban with anger,
'How dare you trick me, I will stay here no longer.'

Jacob now knew what it was like to be cheated,
And he felt unhappy and defeated.
But Uncle Laban wanted Jacob and Leah to stay,
So he told Jacob that there was a way.

As long as Jacob stayed and worked for another
seven year spell,
He could marry Rachel too, so all would be well.
Jacob worked hard for Rachel and Leah;
Then they set out for the home of his mother and
brother.

When they were almost there, he saw his brother
Esau draw near,
And he hurried towards him, starting to fear.
Would Esau try to kill him, should he turn and run?
Or would he forgive him as God had done?

Well, Esau held out his arms and hugged his
brother.
And they cried as they clung to one another.
'I'm sorry,' said Jacob, 'what I did was so wrong.'
'I forgive you,' said Esau, 'now you are back where
you belong.'

Jacob never forgot the lesson he had learned;
The forgiveness of the brother he had spurned.
God knew his plans for Jacob were clearly mapped
out,
And Jacob would obey him for ever, there was no
doubt.

Joseph at Home

Jacob had a very big family.
You would think they could all live happily.
But no, not everyone liked everyone,
Because there was a problem with the youngest one.

Joseph was a favourite and was spoiled,
And never wore a shirt that was soiled.
Because Jacob, who was his father,
Told him to throw it away and he gave him another.

Now his brothers, there were eleven of them,
Looked at each other, and said, 'When
Will our father buy us a new shirt?
We work hard and get covered in dirt.

'Why should our father treat us so,
What is so special about Joseph? We want to know.'
But what really got their goat
Was when Jacob bought Joseph a wonderful coat.

It was made of material, coloured with every hue;
Yellows, greens, reds, oranges and blue.
It was long and soft, the best they'd ever seen,
And the brothers were envious; their faces green.

But there was something else they hated,
And they got together and debated.
'It is all this talk about what he dreams;
He talks about it every day it seems.

'Last night he said he dreamt of bundles of wheat,
And our bundles of wheat bowed down at Joseph's
feet.
And he dreamt that we were all stars in the sky,
And our stars bowed down to his, up on high.

'He acts like a king,' another brother said,
'I don't know what gets into his head.
He needs to be taught a lesson, that is for sure,
Before he drives us all mad, he is such a bore.'

And so when they next went to tend the sheep,
Joseph went with them, without a peep.
When they were out of their father's sight,
They grabbed hold of Joseph and held him tight.

They tore off his coat and threw him down a well,
They might have killed him, who can tell?
But in the distance they saw a cloud of dust
And they ran off quickly as they knew they must.

Along came some traders loaded with goods to sell,
And they heard a noise coming from the well.
They pulled up Joseph all battered and worn;
His shirt all dirty, the sleeves all torn.

'We are going to Egypt,' the traders told him,
And they would take him and trade him in
To be slave and they would get paid.
Twenty pieces of silver; a lot of money to be made.

And when the traders disappeared, taking Joseph
away,
The brothers sang as they went on their way.
They had got rid of their awful spoilt brother,
But what were they going to say to their father?

They thought up a plan and dipped Joseph's coat
Into the blood of a dead goat.
They told Jacob that Joseph was killed by robbers,
And they showed him the coat, all in tatters.

Jacob wept and wept for the son who was gone,
And Joseph wept too, as he was carried along.
He was to be taken far from his home;
Now he had no family and he was alone.

He was sold as a slave to one of the king's men,
He was kind and Joseph worked hard for him.
Potiphar was his master's name and to Joseph he
    gave
The job of being in charge of the slaves.

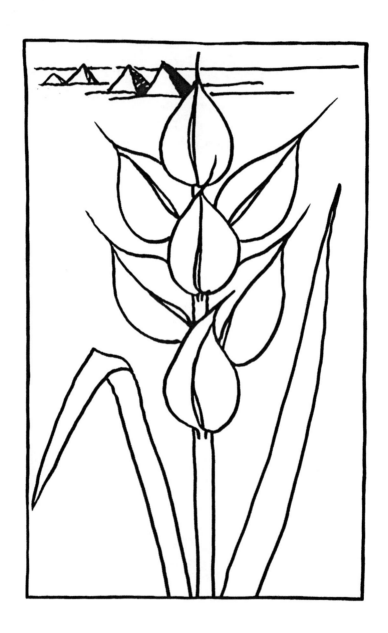

Joseph the Slave

Although Joseph himself was a slave,
It was to Potiphar his loyalty he gave.
But he was hated by Potiphar's wife,
Who wanted Joseph out of their life.

She made up stories that were not true,
Joseph denied them, but what could he do?
He could not tell Potiphar what his wife had done
And so a life in prison was begun.

He still prayed to God every day,
But he found it hard to know what to say.
It seemed now, his dreams would never come true,
But God was watching over him and knew what to
    do.

One of the prisoners had a dream one night,
'Joseph, I saw such a strange sight.
I saw a grapevine with branches – three.
And I couldn't believe just what I could see.

'Grapes burst forth before my eyes;
Beautiful dark purple grapes, dark as night-time
    skies.
I squeezed them into a cup and gave it to the king.
Tell me Joseph, does my dream mean anything?'

Joseph listened carefully and God listened too,
'Now,' God said to Joseph, 'I'll interpret it for you.
This slave once served the king with wine
And in three days all will be fine.

'He will be freed to serve the king once more.'
Joseph told the slave and said he was sure
That this would come to pass, as he foretold,
And that is just what happened, lo and behold!

For two long years Joseph was locked in his cell.
He often thought of his brothers, throwing him in to
    the well.
Then one day a message came from the king,
And Joseph was taken from the prison to stand
    before him.

The king said, 'I had a dream last night,
And I saw a very strange sight.
My wine server said you could explain what it
    means.'
And he described to Joseph the strangest of scenes.

'Seven fat healthy cows were standing by the shore
Happily chewing grass, when they were joined by
    more.
These other cows were scrawny and thin,
And although there was grass, they didn't tuck in.

'Instead they ate the seven plump cows one at a
    time.
But they stayed thin, surely this must be a sign?'
Once again God whispered in Joseph's ear,
'I will tell you what to say, close your eyes and hear.'

Then Joseph told the king what he wanted to know:
There would be seven good years when the crops
    would grow,
And as the sun shone the cattle would grow fat;
The people would prosper because of that.

But Joseph warned the king that the people must put by
Half of the crops that grew, because by and by,
Another seven years would not be so good;
Nothing would grow just as it should.

Unless they saved for the bad days, when there was no sun,
People would die, just as the fat cows had done.
The king was so happy at what Joseph had said,
'You need not go back to prison, look after my store houses instead.'

And so it came to pass and it all came true.
When the crops were harvested, Joseph knew what to do.
Then when the crops failed for the next seven years,
There was plenty to eat, no need for tears.

Joseph became Egypt's most important man,
In fulfilling God's most important plan.
And he prayed and thanked God for making his dreams come true
And telling him always just what to do.

Joseph the Ruler

Joseph became the ruler of Egypt
The very best that that the king had picked.
He had a big house, with servants to wait on him;
When people had problems they came to him.

One day a servant came to Joseph to say,
'There are eleven brothers wanting to speak to you
today.'
'Show them in,' said Joseph, and then before his eyes
Stood his eleven brothers. What a surprise!

The brothers did not recognise Joseph as he looked
so grand,
But why have they come? Joseph thought. *I do not
understand.*
They bowed down before him and fulfilled his long-
ago dream;
His brothers bowing to him, just as he had seen.

'We have come to Egypt from Canaan's land.
We have had no rain, and the fields have turned to
sand.
The people are starving, and dying every day,
We have some money to buy food, we can pay.'

'All right,' said Joseph, 'I will sell you food, as much
as you can hold.
Load up the camels,' his servants were told.
Then he took one of his servants aside,
'I want you to take this silver cup and put it in one
bag to hide.

'Put that bag on the donkey of the youngest boy,'
Said Joseph, who had a plan, and this was his ploy:
When the brothers reached the edge of the town,
Joseph was waiting and he flagged them down.

The bags were searched and they found the cup,
'Right,' said Joseph, 'you stole that cup, the game is
    up!
Now this boy must stay in Egypt and be my slave.'
And he wondered how the others would behave.

'Please don't keep him,' they all said together,
'Keep one of us, but not this young brother.
It would break our father's heart to lose another son.
For many years ago, he lost a beloved one.'

Joseph then revealed to them whom he really was,
And said that he forgave them because
God had told him that he had used their sin
To bring about a wonderful life for him.

'Go now,' he said, 'and fetch my father and mother.'
And he hugged each and every brother.
'God has brought us all together again;
It was all part of a wonderful plan.'

And so it was that Joseph's dreams came true;
They were starting again, as God wanted them to
    do.

Baby in the Basket – Moses

There were too many Israelites in Egypt
And the king decided what he would do about it.
He told his soldiers to kill all the Hebrew baby boys
And all around this caused a great noise.

Mothers were screaming, wailing and crying,
And some held their babies and started running.
There was one baby that God did not want to die;
His mother sat quietly praying as God told her why.

'This is the great, great, great grandson of Abraham,
And I need him to carry out my plan.
Take a wicker basket and make it watertight,
Then take it down to the river in the middle of the
    night.

'Put the baby in the basket and place it in the rushes,
Close to the bank away from where the river gushes.
Let your daughter stay close by him, out of sight,
And he will sleep peacefully all through the night.'

Early next morning a special person came by.
It was the King of Egypt's daughter and she heard a
    baby cry.
Her servant lifted the basket from the water
And showed the baby to the king's daughter.

It was clearly a case of love at first sight
As the princess took the baby and held him tight.
'I don't care if this baby is a Hebrew,
I want to keep him with me, and I know what I will do.

'I must find a woman to be a nurse to him,'
And her eyes were drawn to a nearby bush where his
sister hid within.
She came out of hiding and knelt at the princess's
feet,
'Your Highness, I know a woman I would like you
to meet.'

She took the king's daughter to her mother's house
And the mother was hired to be the baby's nurse.
'I will call him Moses,' the princess said,
And God looked down from heaven and nodded his
head.

Moses would be brought up by his mother
And he would have with him his sister and brother.
They would be brought up as a Hebrew family,
And have a comfortable life, and live happily.

God's plan would not take place for many years to
come
But he knew that Moses was to be his chosen one.

The Burning Bush – Moses

The sun in the desert was very hot;
There was no shade in this spot.
And as the sun's rays beamed down,
They shone on Moses, who was very brown.

Then before him he saw a wonderful sight:
A bush was burning with a bright light.
He stood and watched its colours arrayed,
Red, oranges, yellows and gold displayed.

Moses expected the bush to burn up and disappear
But this didn't happen as Moses stood near.
Instead, it got brighter and brighter with a glowing
    light,
Moses had never seen such a sight.

Then came from the bush a voice,
And Moses knew whose voice he heard.
He knew it was God's voice
And he listened to every word.

'Take off your shoes, Moses.
This is a holy place.
I am here because you have been chosen
From the whole human race.

'I want you to lead the people of Israel from this land.
You must cross these barren lands full of sand.
I want you to take the slaves from Egypt and set
    them free,
Moses will you do this for me?'

Moses trembled and he was very afraid,
But he knew that God's will must be obeyed.
Still he pleaded with God and said he was too old,
And why would the people do as they were told?

'Come,' said God, 'I will show you what you must
   do.
The people will know that I am with you.
Take the walking stick in you hand,
And throw it down on to the land.'

Moses did as he was told and, much to his surprise,
It turned into a serpent, right before his eyes.
'Now pick it up,' said God, and Moses obeyed,
And it turned back into the stick, the one that Moses
   had made.

'When you show the people what you can do,'
Said God, 'they will follow you.'
'But I am afraid,' said Moses, 'to do this alone.'
God spoke quietly, 'Then take your brother Aaron
   with you, my son.'

So Moses replaced his shoes, marked the spot and
   journeyed on
Under the scorching, burning hot sun.
He went to Egypt with Aaron to do as God had said,
To show the way to Israel, the people would be led.

The Great Escape – Moses

When Moses and Aaron reached Egypt, they visited
   the king
And the king asked them what gifts they did bring.
'We bring the word of God, that is all you see.
You are to set his people free.'

The king just laughed and thought it funny,
'You must be mad; my slaves are worth money.
They work hard, so don't you see?
I will never, ever set them free.'

'Then God will punish you,' Moses replied.
And all the water in the river dried.
In place of water blood began to flow,
And frogs appeared from the earth below.

All the dust in the air, and all the sand,
Changed into gnats which flew around.
But still the king would not let the people go;
So flies came, and sickness and sores started to
   grow.

Still the stubborn king refused with a frown;
So from the heavens hail came pouring down.
It battered the crops, and locusts flew in,
And before darkness they had eaten everything.

And the darkness lasted three whole days;
No sign of the sun's bright, golden rays.
And finally God sent an angel to kill the king's son,
So the king gave in; God's will must be done.

'Take your people and leave,' was the king's decree.
So Moses said to the people, 'Follow me.'
And they cheered as they walked towards the river,
Marvelling that God had sent Moses to deliver.

But the king didn't want them to get away,
So he set out with his army to destroy them that
  day.
In front of the people was the sea so deep and flow-
  ing,
And behind was the king's army, so their fear was
  growing.

God spoke to Moses, as he stood on the shore,
'Lift up your stick, and do no more.'
And at once the waves parted, leaving dry land,
And the people ran quickly through the sand.

When they reached the other side,
'God said, lower your stick now, I will turn the tide.'
And the water rushed in and washed the army away,
And they all gave thanks to God for saving them
  that day.

The Long Journey – Moses

The people were grumbling night and day
As they travelled through the desert a long long
  way.
'Where are we going?' the people said,
'We are tired and weary and need to be fed.'

Moses sighed, *What can I do?*
Everything was now in God's hands, that he knew.
He could only lead them back to their special land,
Across the heated desert covered in sand.

They should be glad now that they were finally free,
No longer slaves, but what did he see?
They grumbled with long faces and no smiles,
As they trudged along for miles and miles.

So Moses prayed to God to give them food,
And the quails came in the evening and they tasted
  good.
In the morning the ground was covered in flakes
  called manna,
And the people ate them and sang 'Hosannah!'

Water came from the hard dry rocks for them to
  drink.
This should have made them happy, but what do you
  think?
They mumbled and grumbled once again,
So Moses got cross and called them a pain.

'Why can't you put your trust in God? He will show
    you the way.'
And God sent a fire in the sky at night and cloud to
    follow in the day.
And soon they came to the land he had promised
    them,
The land of Isaac, Jacob and Abraham.

And God took Moses to a mountain, where they
    were alone;
God showed Moses ten commandments written on a
    stone.
'These are the rules the people must obey
And I want you to build a temple where the people
    can pray.'

But the people would not enter the holy land
And God was angry, and sent them back to the sand.
'Forty years you must wander with no place of your
    own.
Forty years and you will be tired of being all alone.'

And after forty years the people repented,
And God saw their plight and he relented.
He led the people into their promised land,
Just as he had originally planned.

And the people sang with joy, and did not moan,
For at last they knew they had come home.

Jericho

God's people of Israel went to Jericho but they could
    not get in;
Moses had died and Joshua had replaced him.
Jericho had a very high wall built all around,
A high strong wall of stone, built very sound.

Joshua marched the people up and down,
'Now how are we to enter?' said Joshua, with a frown.
Suddenly an angel appeared with a sword,
And said, 'Listen, Joshua, I will tell you God's word.'

And as he spoke, he swung the sword around his
    head,
And a plan came to Joshua, and to his men he said,
'We will march around the walls once each day.
We will do this for six days and while we walk we
    pray.'

The people of Jericho couldn't believe their eyes.
They laughed, and said, 'They must be mad; it's a
    trick in disguise.'
They were even more amazed when, on the seventh day,
They marched around seven times in the same way.

By the time they had finished marching they looked
    like tiny spots
Because night had come and they carried lights in
    stone pots.
Then they raised their trumpets and blew for all
    their worth
And the walls of Jericho came tumbling down to earth.

They banged their pots together and blew their
   trumpets loud,
And the army of Jericho fell stunned, all around.
And before Joshua and his army entered the town of
   Jericho,
They sang and danced round and round, putting on
   quite a show.

They sang and as they danced they shouted, 'Hip,
   hip, hurrah!
God has been with us, he showed us the way.'

Gideon

'Gideon, Gideon,' God called one day,
'I need your help. What do you say?'
But Gideon was hiding down in a well,
So God said, 'I know you are there, I can see you
    well.'

'I'm sure,' said Gideon, 'you can't be talking to me.
I am a nobody, I'm a poor weakling, can't you see?'
God said, 'You are not a weak man, you are brave
    and strong.
And I need your help, so please come along.'

'The Midianites have captured my people, and they
    need your aid.
I want you to round up an army, all my plans are
    made.'
So Gideon did as God told him and collected thirty
    thousand men.
'Oh dear,' said God, 'there are far too many of them.

'If my plan is to work send some of them away.'
So Gideon sighed, and tried to hide his dismay.
'The Midianites have more men than I can count.
They will soon wipe my army out.

'You tell me to send away men and yet
I really need all the help that I can get.'
But God insisted and Gideon did as he was told
And sent home the men that were too young, and
    those too old.

At last only ten thousand were left, ready to fight,
But God told Gideon, this still was not right.
'Take them to the river, and get them to drink,
And watch how they do this, and tell me what you
  think.'

Gideon watched as men lapped up the water just
  like dogs that day,
While others scooped up the water in a refined and
  gentle way.
The first he sent for and told them to go away,
While the others with good manners he told to
  stay.

There were only three hundred left now.
How he could win, he didn't know.
'God, there are thousands of Midianites and we are
  so few.
Please God, you will have to tell us what to do.'

'I want you to wait until it is dark,'. God said,
'When all the Midianites have gone to bed.
In one hand all your men must carry a light,
In the other a trumpet to give them a fright.'

When Gideon gave the order all the men blew loud
  and clear,
And they smashed their pots, and oh dear!
They made such a noise, such an awful din;
The Midianites were so confused and they soon
  gave in.

They didn't have time to prepare
And they stumbled and fell everywhere.
They quickly turned and ran away
And God's people won their battle that day.

Hannah's Son – Samuel

Hannah wanted a baby; she wanted a son.
But no baby came, what was to be done?
I will ask God in a prayer,
He will listen if he is there.

'Dear God, I would love a baby of my own.
Please God, give me a son, if only on loan.
Let me have him for a little while,
To hold him close and see his smile.

'I promise that when the time is right,
I will take him in the night
To Shiloh, and the priest called Eli.
This is my word and on it you can rely.'

And so it came to pass that a son was born,
Bringing happiness to Hannah on that morn.
She named him Samuel, a very good name,
One that, one day, would bring him fame.

Hannah kept her promise and when Samuel was a
    very small boy,
She took him to Eli, he was her pride and her joy.
'Eli, one day I made God a vow,
And the time has come to fulfil that promise now.

'Look after Samuel and teach him well.
God may have plans for him, who can tell?'
So Eli took the boy into his home
And grew to love him as his own.

God looked down on the people of Israel
And there were many things he wanted to tell:
How they should be happy and care for each other,
To show kindness to parents, sister and brother.

'I need someone to speak to the people for me.
Now who shall I choose? Let me see.'
And as he looked he saw Samuel in bed fast asleep,
And at Eli in the next room, God did peep.

God called to Samuel, 'Wake up Samuel, it is me
    Samuel.'
Samuel awoke, but all seemed quiet, nothing
    unusual.
It must have been Eli calling to me.
So he got out of bed and went to see.

He shook Eli from his sleep and said,
'Did you want me?' 'No,' said Eli, 'now go back to
    bed.'
But God called again and Samuel ran to Eli,
'You did call me again, now don't deny.'

'You have been dreaming, and hearing voices in
    your head,
Now be a good boy and go back to bed.
Tomorrow I am going to be very busy,
and you are making my head feel dizzy.'

But God spoke to Samuel for a third time
And out of his bed, Samuel did climb.
'Eli, I heard that voice *again*,
I'm sorry to be such a pain!'

'Perhaps,' said Eli, 'God is calling to you.
If he calls again this is what you must do:
Just say, "Please, God, here I am, what do you want
  of me?"
And listen to his answer and perhaps you will see.'

When God once again called Samuel's name,
He told God he was listening and could he explain
What God wanted him to do? What was God's
  plan?
And God told him. 'You will be a very special man.

'I want you to go out among my people.
Teach them right from wrong,
Tell them how to be happy,
And how to get along.

'Tell them not to envy what others have.
To love one another, and to comfort the sad.
Feed those who are hungry, and help to clothe the
  poor;
To nurse the sick, and to make sure
That my chosen people know I will love them ever-
  more.'

And Samuel spent his whole life passing on God's
  word,
And the people listened and remembered what they
  had heard.
And Hannah must have been very proud of her son,
Knowing that through him God's will was being
  done.

David and the Giant

David was a shepherd boy tending the sheep;
Under the stars, David had to sleep.
He came from quite a large family
And had several brothers in the army.

He was always willing to do things to please,
And often at midday he carried bread and cheese
To his brothers, who were defending their town
Against the Philistines, an army of renown.

In the Philistine army was a giant of a man;
Just try and imagine him, if you can.
Goliath was this huge man's name,
And his victories over his enemies brought him fame.

He was over seven feet tall
With a chest like a big stone wall.
He had to stoop down to pass through doors,
And he had huge great hands, like a lion's paws.

When dressed in his armour he was an awesome
    sight;
Enough to give any man a terrible fright.
And his voice was very deep and loud;
He could be heard for miles around.

One day he stood upon some high ground,
And called to David's people who were standing around,
'I dare any one of you to come and fight with me.
If there is anyone brave enough let him come and
    we'll see.'

Now, the boy David heard what Goliath had to
say,
And he knew that God was watching over him
that day.
I will ask the king if I can fight Goliath
And over the Philistines we will triumph.
When the king heard David's request, he was
amazed
At the small boy; the king gazed.
'Why, Goliath is as big and strong as a lion.'
'I know,' said David, 'but I have God to rely on.'

And David picked up five little stones that would
fit in his sling,
And he went to fight the giant, on behalf of the
king.
Goliath roared with laughter when he saw the lad;
This would be the easiest victory he had ever had.

He raised his great spear and came towards the
shepherd boy
But David was ready and he had a ploy.
He placed one of the stones into his sling,
And with a flash of his arm, he gave it a swing.

The stone flew like an arrow through the air
And hit Goliath's forehead – no armour was there.
The huge giant fell dead on the ground,
And a great cheer went up, all around.

The rest of the Philistine army ran away quickly;
For with Goliath dead there would be no victory.
And that is how the saying has been passed to us
all:
'The bigger they are, the harder they fall!'

So David saved the people from their enemy
And the king rewarded him and his family.
And when David grew up, he also became a king,
And God's people rejoiced and their praises did sing.

Solomon

King David ruled for many years
And when he died, there were lots of tears.
He had been a good, kind and holy king,
And had great wisdom about everything.

So David's son Solomon had to take his place;
It was a task that he was afraid to face.
He knelt down and to God he prayed,
And this is the plea that he made:

'Dear God, I do not want riches, no silver or gold;
I do not want beauty to behold.
I just want to live a simple life in peace and har-
mony;
To be a just man, like my father David, you see.'

And God smiled down at Solomon, and nodded his
head,
'You have asked for something very special,' he said.
'For today I give you a gift, to help you live a good
life,
It is wisdom and it will come to your aid in times of
strife.'

Then one day two women came to the king and a
baby they had;
One was holding the baby, the other looked sad.
Each one claiming the baby as their own,
They asked the king to decide who would have it,
While the other would have none.

Solomon knew that this was his testing time,
Now how was he to choose?
Whichever mother he gave the baby to, the other
would lose.
*I will pray for guidance from God, he will tell me what to
do.*
And God whispered, 'You must test the two.'

So he called the two women before him, saying not a
word.
Then he ordered one of his soldiers to take out his
sword.
And taking hold of the baby, he ordered it to be cut
in half,
And the soldier looked at Solomon and gave a nerv-
ous laugh.

But Solomon gave the order for the deed to be carried out
And suddenly one woman stepped forward with a
shout,
'Stop! Please don't kill my baby, let her take it if you
must.'
And Solomon turned to her and the baby at her he
thrust.

'Only a loving mother would give her child away,
To stop it being killed, so I know it is you; now take
it and pray.
Thank God that he answered my prayer, and wisdom he gave to me;
When I needed guidance, he told me how to use it,
you see.'

And Solomon lived many years, and was just and
  kind,
And he used his wisdom when answers he had to
  find.
And every day he thanked God for helping him to
  rule and know
That he was always there watching over him, wher-
  ever he may go.

Jonah and the Whale

Jonah was a miserable man and he always grumbled.
He never agreed with anyone; he just mumbled.
But God watched him, and decided what to do.
'Jonah,' he said, I have a job for you.

'I want you to go to Nineveh, the people there are
  bad.
They are doing lots of nasty things, it is making me
  sad.'
'Oh no!' said Jonah, grumbling in his usual way,
'In fact, God, I was planning on going the opposite
  way.'

'You know those people in Nineveh hate us, and
  what can I do?'
'Just as I ask you,' God replied, 'I will tell you.'
But, still grumbling, Jonah boarded a boat,
Mumbling something about being cold without a
  coat.

The boat wasn't going to Nineveh, but the other
  way;
It was fine and sunny on that summer's day.
But God sent a storm when they were out at sea
And he watched and he knew what he would see.

As the boat tossed and turned even the sailors were
  afraid.
'Oh dear God, help and save us,' they prayed.
But still the boat tossed to and fro
And great waves came up from the sea below.

'God must be very angry,' said one man,
'I do wish he would calm the sea again.'
Just then Jonah called out above the noise,
'It is me that he is angry with, I made the wrong choice.

'Throw me overboard and you will all be saved.'
And as they did as he told them, God commanded the waves.
The sea was calm, the storm abated.
Then God watched and he waited.

Jonah started mumbling and grumbling as the ship sailed away
And he felt himself drowning, what could he say?
If he had done what he had been told
He would not be dying so young; now he would never grow old.

Then Jonah spotted a huge great whale,
With a great big head, and a very large tail.
It was swimming towards him at a very great rate.
'I must get away,' he screamed, but it was too late.

The whale opened its mouth and Jonah floated inside.
It was dark and smelly and Jonah cried.
'I should have gone to Nineveh,' he said,
'Now I'm inside a whale, but at least I'm not dead.'

And so Jonah spent three days asleep,
As the whale swam on through the deep.
Then the whale spat out Jonah onto a sea shore
And Jonah grumbled and mumbled some more.

God spoke to Jonah again and said to him,
'Now go to Nineveh and see the king.
Tell him that in the next forty days,
The people must change their evil ways.'

Jonah obeyed and did as he was told;
And the people of Nineveh repented, young and old.
But still Jonah kept up his mumbling
And God smiled at him, and forgave his grumbling.

Daniel and the Lions

Once again God was feeling sad,
Most of his people were being bad.
They were not obeying any of his laws
And they were fighting each other without cause.

They were stealing things from one another,
They were arguing, sister and brother.
No one was bothering to pray
And no one listened to what God had to say.

God warned them that if they didn't obey,
He would allow their enemies to defeat them one
    day.
Still they didn't listen to what they were told,
So their enemies came and made them slaves as of old.

Now one man called Daniel was a good man,
'God,' he prayed, 'I will help you, if I can.
Perhaps if I talk to the king,
He will listen and could do something.'

Some of the king's men were jealous of Daniel;
The king seemed to like him, this poor menial.
They spied upon Daniel and they heard him pray
To his God, night and day.

They went to see the king, and persuaded him to
    make a decree,
That no one should pray to anyone but he.
And when next morning Daniel knelt in prayer,
His enemies were waiting there.

They grabbed him roughly and dragged him before
the king,
'He has broken your new law, so punish him.
Throw him in the lions' den
And he will not live to disobey you again.'

The king was very sad, but what could he do?
He had passed the law, that was true.
So Daniel was thrown into the lions' cage;
They hadn't been fed for what seemed like an age.

Daniel was very much afraid,
'Please, God, save me,' Daniel prayed.
The lions roared and came towards him growling,
When something happened, quite amazing.

A voice said, 'Sh! Cats, go away,
This man is not your dinner today.'
And the lions lay down, purring gently,
And they licked their paws, quite contently.

Daniel turned to see where the voice had come from
And he saw an angel with a halo on.
A bright light shone all around
And he told Daniel to lay and sleep upon the
ground.

The king had not slept well that night;
What he had done did not feel right.
Daniel had done nothing to deserve to die,
And the king sat down and gave a sigh.

Just then one of the servants ran to the king,
'Sire, I have just seen a most wonderful thing.
Daniel is lying in the cage fast asleep and calm,
While the lions are guarding him from harm.

So the king went and fetched Daniel from the den,
And vowed that his people would be good again.
They would study God's laws and learn to obey
And they would pray to God night and day.

The Great Homecoming

The people had learned their lesson and were good
   once more,
And God was pleased, and what is more,
He decided the time was right for them to go
Back to the land he had given them long ago.

But they were all serving under Cyrus the King,
So God knew that he had to do something.
He spoke to Cyrus, who was kind and good
And Cyrus listened carefully as God knew he would.

'Set my people free,' God said, 'for now is the time
For them to return to Jerusalem, that land of mine.'
And Cyrus obeyed and set them all free
And they made the long journey over the sea.

When they reached Jerusalem there was work to be
   done;
They built houses and a temple where there were
   none.
But there was still so much more to do,
When would it be finished no one knew.

Now Cyrus the King had died and another took his
   place.
And this king had a servant called Neheimiah,
   meaning 'happy face'.
It was Neheimiah's job to serve the king wine
And he had to taste it first to make sure it was fine.

One day Neheimiah looked very sad
And the king asked him if he was feeling bad.
'No,' said Neheimiah, 'I've heard my people are suffering in Jerusalem,
I wish that I could go and help them.

'They have run out of stone and wood
So they can't go on building, even though they should.
The king said he would send Neheimiah with supplies,
And some of his soldiers too, for he was very wise.

Neheimiah thanked the king and they set out for Jerusalem,
The soldiers going along with them.
When they arrived they found the place in an awful state,
But now with the wood and the stone, they couldn't wait.

They started building houses, and a good stone wall
All around, to make it safe for all.
And when they had finished they went to the temple to pray,
Thanking God for all the blessings he gave them every day.

Lightning Source UK Ltd.
Milton Keynes UK
11 August 2010